EXTROSPECTIONS

by Jacob Haddon

Extrospections
Jacob Haddon
all poems copyright 2000, 2015

ISBN 978-1507895184

Cover photograph Josefa Holland-Merten
unsplash.com/hollandmerten

A Sparrow Poetry collection

Table of Contents

The Three Living and the Three Dead Part I — 1

Jazz — 2
Blues — 3
Time — 4
CrLaOiUnD — 5
Ceiling Tiles — 6
Notes, women, fish, lines, notes, and Carrie Anne — 7
Signs — 9

The Three Living and the Three Dead Part II — 11

Extrospection — 12
B-sides — 13
Lucid — 14
Name — 15
The Restaurant at Asnieres (1887) — 16
Coffee Break — 17
Brake — 18
The Stairwell — 19

The Three Living and the Three Dead Part III — 20

Earthquake — 21
Communion — 22
Reading — 23
Two — 24
Fork in the Road — 25
Rock — 26

The Three Living and the Three Dead Part IV	27
Pygmalion	28
Phaeton	29
Samson	30
The Persecutors	31
Orpheus	32
Charon	34
Hector	35
Number 8	37
Catullus VIII	38
The Three Living and The Three Dead Part V	39
History	40
The End of the Stairwell	41
Night Swimming	42
Relativity	43
St. Christopher	46
Again	48
Park Bench	49
The Three Living and the Three Dead Part VI	51
Good Friday	52
Prelude	54
A crow spoke to me today	55
Author's Afterward	56
About the Author	57

For Kelly

*who helped arrange these poems
all those years ago*

The Three Living and the Three Dead
Part I

The Three Living

The sun hasn't risen for days now.
Every so often, the sky pinkens,
teasing the idea of sunrise.
Only the moon, with its silver dawn,
illuminates. And the cold,
a cold I have never known.
Wrapped heel to ear,
only my eyes show
and my body shivers.
The merchant paces,
his path crosses our camp
in every conceivable way.
He thinks of a woman,
a lady, I presume,
convinced that the forces that hide the sun
will keep them apart.
The knight rests his hand
on his chin,
untrained in dealing with enemies
on the inside,
he has not moved since the now embers
were first set ablaze.
And still there is no dawn.

Jazz

the air is slow thick—people move street to street shop to shop
the city moves never stops never pauses never stays still
forward, leftward, rightward, onward, in, out, around
the change becomes dark bright full of color and nothingness
and still there is motion still there is motion still there is motion
what street is this? what day am I?

this woman who stares into my eyes dares to know something I cannot
    take off at night
and still she is close close moving we move
move until I cannot tell you which moves or how anymore
they move forward onward, she holds my hand
never speaks never speaks only communicates
and I only listen, I listen to her body, her body, her body
and how she moves, when she moves, if she moves

my thoughts swim on motion, motion from here to there
from streetlights and city, through thick air, street to street
a horn plays, "Miles Davis" she whispers, her lips press
and we move, she gently touches my lips apart moving again
onwards, forwards awaywards—but my motion is gone
to me motion only hugs holds keeps, she is in control of motion

I move around anywards her thick kiss motionless on my lips
her motion thick on my body, and I move down down down
until I am a stool, base for a lone trumpet and its motionless freedom

Blues

Lord don't make me sit here all my life
I ain't done you no wrong
Lord don't make me sit here forever
I ain't done you no wrong
Boss-man come along
Take away my song

Lord my eyes hurt from working
Take this machine 'way from me
Lord my hands hurt from working
Take this machine 'way from me
Rain clouds are a-coming
Leaving their rain with me

When five o'clock come
I gonna hit that door
when five o'clock come
I'm gonna lite a smoke
Baby I never saw a more beautiful sun
as the sun after five o'clock come.

Lord I need salvation
This job ain't no good
Lord I need salvation
This world ain't no good
Show me something better
Something better for me.

Time

Walk talk the tic tock, if you have the time
spit trick only wants your tick chick
and to kick tock you to the fuck rut. The sound

of the sip tock goes tick, the gun, click click click,
stops the scene, the clock block knows.
Sphinx says "never forget tic!" the me-mick runs

and you can run, through click ticks, rock
lochs, and all the tick tocks you want, but
the nick knock of time is never there.
Sphinx says "this is no trick!" or truck to the tic

tock clock still ticking ticking. Even a block brick
can destroy the tock time clock, or a wok wick

of a candlestick can burn burn burn though all,
the top clock cares not. It will tick. You will tock,
and the tic tic humans will walk the tock tic
through time. The epoch of it all flick flocks

the mind, letting you cock kick yourself for the tic
of your toc, now side-riding the aftershock.
Sphinx says "phuc tock it! four, two, three!"

His walk, Morning-dAy-eveNing, talk
is to pick poc the click, opening the lock tic,
so I too may tic(R) tic(U) tock(N)

CrLaOiUnD

        rain fell
        rain fell
        rain fell
        rain fell
        rain fell
        rain fell
        rain fell
        rain fell
        rain fell
        rain fell

      dANd   d
        I   aNd
        L   i
       io   lio
       N   n

Ceiling Tiles

There are 169 full ones
Plus a row of 18 halves.
And a quarter tile in the corner.

88 of them flow left to right
87 flow up to down,
Leaving three which appear to go
Diagonal.

The ceiling fan takes the place
Of one, carving curves
Into an adjacent pair.

The ones above the fish tank
Possess ceaseless motion
And the ones near the mirror are reflected out to the imperfections of the glass.

Bringing the total to 178 1/4
Ceiling tiles
And one set of eyes.

Notes, women, fish, lines, notes, and Carrie Anne

I write to explore. the lines
Offer help when women
Dream of animals. Fish
Drink, not just breathe. Friends
Sing of life and Carrie Anne, who
Hears clearly the notes.

I hear clearly what the notes
Write. To explore the lines,
Sing of life and Carrie Anne, who
Offers help when women
Drink, not just breathe. Friends,
Dream of animals, fish.

I dream of animals, fish, and
Hear clearly that the notes
Drink not just breathe. Friends
Write to explore, the lines
Offer help when women
Sing of life and Carrie Anne.

I sing of life and Carrie Anne, who
Dreams of animals. Fish
Offer to help when women
Hear clearly that the notes
Write to explore. The lines
Drink not just breathe, friends.

I drink, not just breathe. Friends
Sing of life and Carrie Anne, who
Writes to explore the line
Dreams of animals. Fish
Hear clearly that the notes
Offer to help women.

I offer help when women
Drink. Do not just breathe, friends,
Hear clearly that the notes
Sing of life, and Carrie Anne who
Dreams of animals. Fish
Write to explore the lines.

I write lines that offer women
Dreams of fish, drinks to thirsty friends
I sing of Carrie Anne, and she hears the notes.

Signs

beware of dog
employees must wash hands
surgeon general's warning

police line—do not cross
no trespassing
no forgiveness for those who trespass against us

in case of emergency—Panic
Don't Panic
remain calm and in your seats
did I not instruct that box five was to be left empty?

you must be 18 or older to purchase tickets
you must be at least this tall to ride

wet paint
only you can start forest fires
abandon all hope
no stopping standing or sitting

fire lane
handicap parking only
employees only
students only
coat and tie required

no posting

no smoking

no food or drink inside library

no sandals or bare feet on the escalator

made in china

made in korea

made in taiwan

inspected by #13

buckle up for your safety

The Three Living and the Three Dead
Part II

The Merchant

The merchant turned,
his expression breaking the silence
before his words.
"Her name," he began,
the cold pouring from his mouth,
"was almost as beautiful
as she.
In the ballroom of the Queen
we met, the masquerade hiding
my wonderment.
Her peers saw my status,
her eyes just saw my own.
I left to make my fortune
in Babylon,
so I may stand at her side
in court."

Extrospection

It was a poet's dream,
memories that will fill
passion and plain white pages.
Recollections of a few months and a single
je t'aime.

I am no poet
a farmer of words, engineer of thoughts
and events, I could not fill a
page.

Yo no soy poeta
a single moment of clarity,
I dwell on the past
like a Romantic
lost in the short walk from home.

I cannot tell you,
for the only thing that is true
is that in the summertime my lips
turn *azul* when I stay in the cold water
too long, all else
  fabri(fabrications)cations

B-sides

My stomach hurts.
It matches rhythm with the ringing
in the top speaker of the hand set.
'Its just coffee" I think,
counting,
15
"Too much caffeine,"
16
"not enough food."
17
I place the receiver back
slowly running my hand down the chord,
and waited for my body to calm itself.

Lucid

I dreamed of you last night.
After an alternative ending,
we walked out of a theatre.
At the top of the escalator
you said goodbye,
and kissed me,
and kissed me,
so much that I knew—
but did not awaken.

The most recent of a series
Each night I fear the feelings
you only show in my sleep.
And each morning
I wake up tired.

Name

His name sent me walking;
my body moving to catch
my thoughts.
I found myself by the huge fountain
near the library.

I light a smoke,
bringing it to my lipless mouth.
My ocular cavities
stare at nothing in particular.

I run my fingers through the water,
wiping the cold against my face
trying not to think of whose hands
touch his face.

The Restaurant at Asnieres (1887)

That tree outside was a sapling
the day I left my Van Gogh.
The year escapes me now.

Now, I sit and watch
the restaurant at Asnieres.

The waitress takes orders,
serves drinks.
Moving table to table.

The yellow door behind her,
open just a crack;
the sounds of remembrance
drifting into the street.

Coffee Break

The waitress here is beautiful
"What can I get you?" she asks.
At first
my voice doesn't work.
"I'm fine," then
"Can I use a pen?"
Though the short dress
is distracting to the eye,
my thoughts fall on the chair
and the empty glass in front of me,
my second,
which attracts the waitress
again
to my table.

Brake

Slowly I walk from your car,
the lights shine at my feet.
Each step from you is matched
by the bodiless feet of
the shadow.
\<PoP\>
Emergency brake is pulled
and the light moves
taking the shadow, and
the chance to retrace our shared path.
As your car leaves, I
remember when the brake was broken
 and I waited till you pulled it
  before walking away. I
Remember when there were kisses goodnight,
 and I waited till you pulled away
  before walking away. I
remember, before the shadow
before the
\<PoP\>
that there was something
to walk away from.

The Stairwell

up—
  each concrete increment
tipped with white
  is one step closer
to the four walls
  that enclose me when I sleep.

down—
  each concrete decrement
tipped with white
  leads back
to the four walls
  from which I ran to here.

time—
  12:51 am

which way?

The Three Living and the Three Dead
Part III

The Knight

The knight began speaking
without lifting his head.
"Once, nobility could be judged
against the knights of my home.
My father said to me
'Only fight for what you will die for.'
And I did.
On that last campaign
pushing through Germany,
our swords were ordered
upon the villages.
I turned, setting out for Babylon,
for the chance to honor a code
that others have forgotten."

Earthquake

You learn a lot about houses
when you live with earthquakes.

The engineer said the houses in Umbria
were built like oak trees, the roots deep
and the material flexible. The houses
that is, except for 104 Church St.

The basilica of St. Francis fell in an earthquake.
The cause was not the design, but
"storage" of waste rubble between
the vaulted ceilings and the outer walls.

My pine home fell in an earthquake.
The cause was not the design, but
The sacrifice of the foundation to
complete the facade under budget.

The ceilings of Assisi are in pieces
just as my home is in pieces
because an architect
never imagined a 4.5 possible.

Communion

I throw back sugar packets
like espresso shots,
crunching crystal sweet
in remembrance of you.

You would have asked
"What the hell?"
if you could hear my thoughts,
and I would have just shrugged.

Instead you compare apple jets
with rocket oranges
and nothing made sense.
"So do you love me yet?"

I nod.

"Liar," you say,
placing a cookie in my mouth;
"I know you."

I grab your shoulders
first the left
then the right

You are the one with wings.

Reading

I sit quietly in the folding chair,
listening to her read her newest. As
she pushes a small lock from her face,
I wonder what it will be like

when I fall in love with this poet
who is better than I am.
I can imagine her reading as I cook,
the two of us discussing the small details

of "a" and "the." She will point out
that I am too dramatic with endings,
and that I never use enough oregano.
I will tell her she drives images too hard,

like her car, which is still in the shop.
(The mechanic called.) "Besides," I'll say,
"what's wrong with a little drama?"
She will tell me of the trip to Chicago

and that one of the poets remembered me
from class in college, and had asked about
life as an engineer. I will kiss her,
and say, "Dinner is ready."

Two

I raise the blade to eye level
checking the quality.

News reflects off the inside of my skull
traveling across to the other
side, reflecting again.

angle of incidence
equals
angel of reflectance

I run the blade under hot water
then up my dry neck

two engagements
one—
    the girl I wanted forever with
the other—
    the girl forever was too short for

my cheek stings, saltwater runs
down
onto a cut
again, blade under hot water
then traced along the other side.

My mask complete, I go downstairs
turning the light off
behind me.

Fork in the Road

I am sitting where the path breaks
in two.
I eat the French fries that are all
that remain of lunch.
One hand taps a pen
against hard ground.
Above, clouds form
shapes too complicated for
simile, and I realize
I am contemplating nothing.
Sphinx says: "Watch for aliens,
somebody made me."
I swallow the last fry,
sand pyramids are too strange for God.
I jump up

Leaving warm ground,
and a fresh picked cherry blossom.

And dance around my little spot

to the rhythm of my hand from before.
Gripping hard one last time,
I throw the pen between the split
path.
Then I turn, setting out
into the uncut field.

Rock

the rock burns in my hand
smooth on smooth, I feel its heartbeat
tighter tighter until bone and rock, mineral against mineral
it is here, writing, I am encompassed by a warm hand

it is gray, it feels gray as I feel human
it moves, it wants to be alive and I sit and write wanting to exist
beyond my body, to live as a rock, starting as a mountain, only to
    become
a beach, spread , a 100 billion of myselves—
soft in abundance, hard in singularity

it is smooth, it has known rivers
it asks what is the sun, who I am, am I a god?
I ask it what is a river, are you a god?
the rock's heartbeat increases
it demands a sense other than temperature

it will not surrender
I will not surrender

only the sky will change, noon, midnight,
the moon is the only constant, without air
without rivers, no rock would be as smooth as the one
that holds me in its hand, no rock would feel "river" or "snow"
only space, where rocks come from
the rock says look at me, I've earned that.

you open your hand, I'll open mine

The Three Living and the Three Dead
Part IV

The Thief

The eyes turned to me.
Their stare overpowered
my reluctance.
"The idea of a thing
that cannot be mine
is too foreign for translation.
A knife can convince a bird
to hand over its wings."
I stir the fire
not meeting their eyes
not wanting their judgment.
"In Babylon I search for
what cannot be stolen."

Pygmalion

I have you now, Pygmalion.
You turn your eyes from woman,
worshiping art as your patron.

Marble peeled away, revealing
her perfection underneath.
But your Galetea is stone.

Weep at her feet.
Then I will listen, when you understand,
I am not a vengeful goddess.

Now kiss her, Pygmalion, kiss her warm lips
And know that without me
You are only marble.

Phaeton

It had just rained
yet the eerie calm still remained.

There must be more clouds on their way.

Daddy, I had the reigns,
every horse under the hood
controlled,
I promise.

But there was water
covering the dark pavement.

No—that's setting
not an excuse.

I drove the horses too hard—
too fast

The brakes locked
and I heard thunder.
But light travels faster than sound

and an object in motion will stay in motion.
Not even the son of a god

can break the law.

Samson

I tried to cut you
out of my head.

I went for the hair, chopping
the ends that entwined with yours,
leaving the newer bases.

Next was the bleach,
stripping color and shape,
leaving only blonde.

But already roots,
brown and thick,
grow from my scalp,

proving that this too
is just part of a mask.

The Persecutors

After leaving Daniel,
the lions came to my home.
Their manes had grown soft
their eyes gray
paws tired of arena sand.

Twice a day they walked me
stopping to see the neighbors
At home we talked of politics in Rome
and the lions all agreed
Hannibal was indeed at the gates.

The lions assured me—
this is just a visit, my friend.
and though I tried to keep them
they insisted—
We must,
there is more work
for the persecutors

Orpheus

I.
Who is this man?
How is it he can compose whole
Sentences with just a single string?
He draws me with music, closer than
A husband should.

II.
Who is this man that
Wakes me for this? The woman
He brings could not be saved
By Aesclapeus himself, the poison
So set on its path.

III.
Who is this man, wandering
Into the under-realm, a lyre
Armed? His voice is his bribe
And yet I still let him
Pass.

VI.
Who is this man stopping
Hell with a single vibration?
When played I forgot this rock
And the worn path, that he too
Will learn.

V.

Who is this man, standing
Before my husband, pleading with
The rhetoric of Cicero? His song will
Remind the dark Lord, that he too
Once fought the gods.

VI.

Who is this man, trying
To change what the fates
Decide? He will turn before
It is time, and the council of
Cassandra, unheard.

VII.

Who is this man, entering
The globe of my lantern from the
Dark? His hand shakes, the grip
on a piece of ripped fabric
So tight.

Charon

I sit in the back of a metal boat,
a gold coin on my tongue,
a fiberglass fishing pole in my hands.

It has been raining for almost
ten minutes, and my father
begins to row.

Through the tumult
I watch the bobber trailing
behind, bow waves arching

into the dancing water,
determined to catch one fish
before the skeleton at the oars

takes me to safety.

Hector

I may wear the armor,
But the god stands before me.
Already poets are composing,
Noting the breeze from the sea,
And the unpolished plate on my shoulder.
I stand before the walls of Troy,
Before my family watching.
Achilles, raising his sword,
Speaks "For Patroclus!"
Clotho wove the threads.

Full force we engage,
A precise thrust glides
Into his shoulder, he
Is unfazed. Strike—my shield breaks,
I thrust, the point breaking the surface of his back.
He pulls the blade
From its flesh sheath,
There is no blood.
Lachesis measures the threads.

Thrice passed the closed gate, my sword
Never far from my shadow.
On my hands and knees I recognize
This patch of earth, a faint memory of
A young Hector and siblings playing here.
Cuts on leather straps,
The armor slides down.
The point of my sword
Guides my head upwards.
On the wall behind, Paris draws his bow.
"Together Achilles," I yell, "We shall go together!"
Atropos cut.

For the love of Helen, a thousand ships, the fallen walls
   of Troy, a royal house, save Aeneas, slain, and a silhouette
   of a wooden horse stained upon history.

Number 8

Poor Jacob, it is time to stop this nonsense
Acknowledge the lost as lost.
Today the sun shines for those
Who possess the damned "L" word,
Walking together, fingers locked.
Places, here, there, are now

Full of thick air and colorless light.
No longer think that time is here.
She wants this no more.
You are Mad, listen to me!
Valete! Tell the bundle of clichés that rise
To your fingertips, you are strong.

Farewell, my Olivia, your Jacob is strong.
Who will you run to? Who will read
Your unfinished poetry, laughing at
Your high diction and poor punctuation?
Whose hand will you find in the night?
Whose tears will find safety on your lips?
You are gone, and your Jacob *est vale*.

Poor Jacob, you speak only to yourself.

Catullus VIII

Poor Catullus, stop this nonsense
And account what you see to be lost as lost.
Once the sun shown bright for you
When you went where your mistress led
Loved by us surpassed by no other who was loved.
There and then gave us many joys

Which you wanted, nor did your mistress not want them.
Those days truly shown bright for you.
Now she wants this no more
To this you are powerless,
Nor should you follow who flees, nor live in misery,
But with a strong mind, endure.

Farewell, woman, your Catullus is strong.
He will not seek you, or ask for you uninvited.
And you will regret, when you can ask no one?
Poor miserable creature, what life is left for you?
Who now will visit you? To whom will you be beautiful?
Who now will you love? Who will you say that you are?
Who will you kiss? Whose lips will you bite?

And you, Catullus, live strong, and endure.

The Three Living and The Three Dead
Part V

The Three Dead

In the distance,
light turned our path.
A lantern sat on a stump
illuminating a pair of trios.
Three skeletons sat in a row.
The first spoke, his right arm
severed in his lap, sword in hand,
"As ye are, so once we were,
and as we are, so shall ye be."
The second spoke, his bones
adorned with barnacles
seaweed draped on ribs and limbs,
a pouch of silver by his side,
"The rich die as well as poor."
The third spoke, a knife
and a noose his possessions,
"None shall escape death."
The lantern went out.

History

Patrick holds up the shamrock
"one, two, three
don't you get it?"

I look at the plant

"You have to taste green
to be Irish.
You must know what iron smells like,
and the hiss of a snake."

I take the the clover from his hand
spinning it about its stalk.
Why green?
Red can mean anything.

"Dream of bronze statues, boy
but, lose your way
and memory will be your sin."

The End of the Stairwell

I sit in the stairwell,
between your room and mine
a dreamer

locked between two floors
full of moments
and the smell of concrete

where I know who I love
where even if I lose
even if I go through that door

and run up those six flights
covering my body with blankets
I will awaken with you in my arms.

All I want is to wake up
but I am so afraid to fall asleep
afraid this time will be different

afraid that in this stairwell
some other room, some other bed
will call you to rest.

And I will awaken,
at the end of a cold stairwell,
with nothing more than sixty

white tipped increments.

Night Swimming

Holding you in the water
I pulled your shivering body
next to mine.

You, troubled by the sight
of a man in a window
on the way to the beach

and me, too worried about you
to notice whether the phantom
lived in a second story room

or the bay water within
arm's reach.

Relativity

I think Einstein had something.
Time depends on velocity of a particle
and the frame of reference.

Five minutes.
Three hundred seconds.

Train station—early 1910's
Colors are alive with subtlety,
the once paint on the station has faded
and the white wash has started chipping.

Two people stand close,
eyes shyly return
hands never far.
Quietly they whisper good-byes
and other three word phrases.

Not far a man stands in a long maroon coat
and a black Stetson hat.
His black leather hands hold a pocket watch.

The bell sounds, train to arrive
Five minutes

The man checks his watch
Four minutes, thirty seconds.
He begins to pace up and down,
cautiously peering over the track.
He checks his watch
Four minutes, ten seconds
Paces more
stops, reads an advertisement
Three minutes, forty-five seconds

He glances at the lovers,
thinking of the day his son left
and how long he had held him
Two minutes, fifty-seven seconds
There was war in Europe
and it was calling his son,
only allowing a stopover
Two minutes, five seconds
It was the right thing
it was the good thing,
he was proud of his son
One minute, fifty-one seconds

The couple pulls into a kiss

The man remembers loving a woman
and tries not to stare
the watch pops open
One minute, ten seconds

the train is in view,
smoke pours from the top
coating the already-black
Fifty-seven seconds
the announcer begins to talk

Thirty-three seconds
Twenty-one seconds
Fifteen seconds
Seven seconds

Time

St. Christopher

Five stand at the dock.
With firm grip on my baggage,
I pull out a cigarette.
Yamato gives me a light.
The ship pulls in, there is
An announcement:
"The Eagle has landed."
We head up the plank,
Buzz turns to me,
"May be a small step for you,
I'm only 5'10"."

The Argos has been at sea
three days now.
I dangle my feet over the railing,
Lady Zillith continues on about why
Sex is better with her on top.
I stare out over the Sea of Tranquility,
thinking of how easily I have forgotten
what "green" means.

Zeroes fly overhead, and we
wave the samurai
off to battle,
praying against mushroom clouds
and bad weather.
"You boys come home,"
Yamato says into a radio.
Buzz looks at me, and points,
"Shouldn't you put your bag down?"

The forty days ended three days ago
and the deck is finally dry.
A crow drops a page in front of me,
blank.
It caws obsessively as it flies away.
Edgar pats my shoulder.
"Don't worry," he says, lighting a smoke,
"They were ravens for me."

The ship bell sounds the hour
12:51
Yamato and Buzz hit golf balls
from the rear deck, arguing
The Kennedy Assassination.
Edgar volunteered to test
Lady Zillith's theories,
the experiment entering hour four.
I toss my baggage over the side.

For four score and seven days,
the wind has blown our ship.
On the horizon Mons Olympus breaks
the sea, and we
Buzz
Edgar
Lady Zillith
Yamato
and myself,
prepare to go ashore.

Again

If I stopped by late
    again
walking the quarter-hour
from my door to yours
    again
bringing my interest in
your day
and a can of Dr Pepper
could you
    again
look at me the way
from a cold night
on top of a parking garage
when you stood high on the edge
to be tall enough to
reach me?

Park Bench

I look into the most beautiful blue eyes
I have ever seen
and understand how anyone can love

"No," I reply to a girl
"He isn't my son."
"He has beautiful eyes." she says

I can understand why he wants so much
to be your father

"Are you friends of the parents?"

I look into those blues again
thinking how the man I call Bill,
and this two year old calls da-da
was the right amount of love
at the wrong time
for a single mother.

They are no longer together,
but those blues still say da-da
and Bill still loves him

"Yes," I say, "I am."
"Does he look like mommy
or daddy?"
The boy reaches out to my nose
"beep."
"His mommy," I say.
"She must be very beautiful."
"That she is, that she is."

The Three Living and the Three Dead
Part VI

The Dawn

The sun rose each morning after
our paths turned from Babylon.
Soon the Mediterranean climate returned
and we stripped off the layers
added to protect our bodies.
The knight set his feet
for conquered lands. Wielding
a hammer, the Carpenter
battled something
worth dying for.
The merchant looked beyond station,
the Priest used wealth as a means
not an end.
I picked up a pen
to tell everyone
directions to Babylon.
Memento Mori.

   -The Poet

Good Friday

I wake up
and I have lost my voice.
Light bent by clouds
causes shadows to creep along
the floor. In the hallway
men with white collars fold
a curtain which has ripped in two
this morning.

Outside a woman kneels over a tape
outline, clawing at the
pavement.

A ghost wanders, unable to
see his mother.

Picking a cherry blossom,
I continue on my way, thinking
this flower used to be white
and I could talk,
till this morning.

The boy-spirit follows, we pass by a
dogwood. All the petals without pink
have fallen, making a mosaic with
no discernable pattern.

From above,
oak seeds fall
in a great swarm
cutting through the dogwood
taking white petals with them.

The spirit reaches out, but the choppers
fall unheeded
through his open hand.

Prelude

Light is always colored in a church.

You really fucked up this time, Orpheus.

Up, down, in, out; make up your mind.

She is in all white, moving up the main isle.

There is music, I know there is music.

Hades stands at the end, unconcerned with a simple living boy.

Places in our past haunt us, they are ghosts for the sane.

Her breasts are pressed against me, she is asleep

I am awake.

Now she is on the other side of the room.

Now she is on the other end of the phone.

No choice of words can prepare you for the sunlight.

A crow spoke to me today

A crow spoke to me today
as I walked by its perch.
The black of its feathers clashed
   against the new color on the branch
   recently awoken by spring.

The bird spoke, but I did not understand,
just continued to walk
a darkening sky filled my thoughts.

The crow called out again
with more urgency,
calling out over the distance between us.

I glanced over my shoulder
at the black staring at me,
not breaking pace,
fearing impending rain.

For a third and final time,
the crow spoke.
It screamed its message aloud,

but I continued on
not stopping to listen to this little Iris,
not caring that I would wish
I had listened.

Author's Afterward

Hello.

    This collection of poems is a slice of my past. Collected for a contest judged my senior year of college, this file has collected e-dust on hard drive after hard drive as I moved, graduated, moved again, converted back to a Mac guy, and moved again.

    In 2000, in the halls of the English building at College Park, Maryland, I saw a posted flyer for a book contest judged by one of my favorite poets, Li Young Lee. I decided to take the chance and put together something to submit, not in hopes of winning and getting published, but in hopes that Lee would read my work.

    I printed out a stack of my poems and with the help of my friend Kelly and her entire living room floor we arranged, and mercilessly edited. This collection is the final result. Since then, some have been edited, altered or reverted; I am not sure the tinkering process ever really stops. But this file, this collection stood untouched all these years.

    I present this collection to you unedited, unaltered from all those days ago. Enjoy.

    -jacob
    2010

About the Author

Jacob Haddon is a distracted writer who spends his days pretending to be an engineer. He has been writing poetry since high school, inspired by the Latin poet, Catullus.

You can find him online at jacobhaddon.com

Made in the USA
Middletown, DE
19 July 2015